Printed in the United States of America

First Printing, 2023

ISBN: 979-8-218-30339-6

For more information, visit: https://yolandaharper.com/

I want to start by saying welcome to you and your heart. I am so glad you are in this space. The idea behind this journal is to help you craft time and space to be with your heart, body, mind and soul and to explore some of the concepts from the book Soul Sabbatical – A Journey to Revive the Heart.

You might not consider yourself a "journaler", so I invite you to give yourself permission to use this space as it best suits you. Allow yourself to write in stream-of-consciousness, without worrying about grammar or editing. Write in lists or bullet-points. You can also doodle or color or draw – whatever feels good to you. Take breaks anytime something feels like a lot. Allow this to be an environment where you meet yourself with nurture and respect – especially in the places you are least comfortable.

Write yourself a reminder that it is in this sense of spaciousness, trust, and allowing that you'll become acquainted again (or for the first time) to your heart. And that's where the magic happens. And how you craft your own life of a Soul Sabbatical.

I believe in you and your heart. Oh, and I'm so proud of you. What might feel like uncertainty, risk, and emotional exposure is one of the most brave things any of us can do.

From my heart to yours,
Yolanda

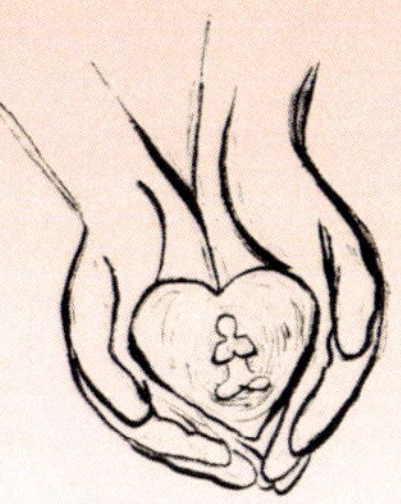

Lead with your Heart

Let's start with an introduction!

Use the space on this page to explain who you are.
Whether it is with words, paint, or magazine cut-outs,
make it uniquely YOU!

What else is true about you that is lost if Hustle-You is the only one making introductions?

🌼 Dear Hustle-You...

Let's face it, Hustle-You has served an important purpose in your life. But it's time to start putting some limits on her.

Use the space below to write a letter to Hustle-You. You can use the following format:

Dear Hustle-Me,

Thank you for all you have done for me...
These are the things you have given me...
These are the things you have cost me...

It's time for things to look different now.
Love,

Chapter 1: The Great Resignation

Maybe the thought has tickled your mind and
quickened your heart. We do get a choice to quit.
Think with your mind, but even more, take a breath
deep into your heart.
What is the first thing you'd like to resign from, if you
could choose something?

When you're ready, write a letter of resignation

Repeat this process as many times as you need.

To the patriarchy

To hyper-capitalism

To perfectionism

To imposter syndrome

To your itty bitty shitty committee

To any other "ism" that has caused damage to your heart

Let's **STOP** apologizing for Being Human

Truly pause at this moment and think of the times that you didn't allow yourself to be human. How different would your life be if you actually acknowledged and honored your physical, human limitations instead of apologizing for them? How different would our planet be if we all did so?

Journal about the ways that you deny your own human needs.

1. Where did you learn to do this?

2. What has it cost you?

3. What would your day look and feel like if you chose ONE thing to do differently?

4. What's one thing you're proud of or thankful for about your body?

Your Heart is Invited to Integration:

What would you like to carry forward from
this chapter into the days of your life?

Chapter 2: The Water We Swim In

<u>FOOBS Fighting</u>
What's your origin story?

Many of us don't necessarily relate to the term "trauma" when we think about our childhoods. But when we look at the ways that we were or weren't, nurtured, guided, and had limits set for us, we have a different understanding of how we learned to exist in the world.

What was your family role?

Circle the role you most identify with.

Hero Child　　　*Scapegoat*　　　*Lost Child*

How has your origin story led to the creation of Hustle-You?

In the box below draw how it felt to be that role...

Your Unexplored Inner Landscape

What parts of you feel "difficult", "dangerous", and "unuseful"?
How does the light and darkness of who you are weave through your heart?

What can you (lovingly) call your shadow self? Jot some ideas down below:

Now that you are becoming acquainted with this part, really create some space for yourself to write a most tender letter to that part. Take your time and be gentle. Take breaks as you need them. Whatever you need to do to listen to your heart and hear what she needs.

The following format might help you:

Dear "Shadow Self"
Thank you for all you have done for me...
These are the things you have given me...
These are the things you have cost me...
It's time for things to look different now.
Love,
(Your name)

What would you like to carry forward from
this chapter into the days of your life?

Chapter 3: Your Heart Has Been Swimming In... Your Heart is Invited To...

Now that we've put words to the truth of what our hearts have been swimming in, let's explore...

What is your heart questioning?

What emotions is your heart experiencing?

Use the space below to explore these emotions with whatever medium you prefer

You can write, draw, collage, paint, or use whatever else you'd like to express yourself.

Create a Journal Entry

Journal about your experiences of *Comparison -> Resentment -> Scarcity. Grief. / Vulnerability. / Shame.*

Do you know Hope? How were you introduced to her?

Hope

Insert a photo of you when you felt hopeful

Your Heart is Invited to Integration:

What would you like to carry forward
from this chapter into the days of your life?

Chapter 4: Permission to Dream

Settle into a quiet space and take a few deep breaths. Now picture what a Perfect Day would look like for you in as much detail as possible. It doesn't have to be a special day of vacation, just a perfect "normal" day.

Now use the rest of the page to create a scrapbook collage of your Perfect Day

Cut up magazines, print photos online, find stickers you have & create your master piece!

How Do You Want to Feel?

Instead of focusing on what I was going to **DO** during my sabbatical, I journaled about how I wanted to **FEEL** at the end of the sabbatical time.

How would you like your days to FEEL?
Use one word below to describe that feeling.

What are the activities that help you feel that way?
Name 4 activities below that help you.

How can you incorporate this into your life more?

1. ____

2. ____

3. ____

4. ____

Your Heart is Invited to Integration:

What would you like to carry forward from
this chapter into the days of your life?

Chapter 5: Exquisite Kindness

Whose Opinions of You Matter

Want to find your people?

In the square below, write down the names of the people whose opinions of you matter.

The people who cheer you on, who are your biggest supporters, but who are also real with you and willing to lovingly hold you accountable (because we're human and sometimes drop the ball and can sometimes be a jerk).

The people that love you not in spite of your imperfections, your quirks, and your idiosyncrasies but because of them.

These should not be a ton of people.

These should fit in your box.

This list?

These are your people

Keep this list close by so that you can remind yourself of who your people are when you realize you're too much for some people.

Your people will love all of you

Concentric Circles of Relationships

Sometimes it's hard to know what parts of your life to share with what people. <u>This can help give you an idea</u>:

1. Fill the people from your box above into the center circle.

2. In the next circle, fill in friends and family who are an important part of your life, but don't belong in the inner circle. You'll notice that this circle holds more people, but the people here have not earned the right to direct access to your heart.

3. The outer circle is for those friends and family who you know and even like, but your only interactions with them are on social media or when they need something from you. These people do NOT get to input on your heart and life.

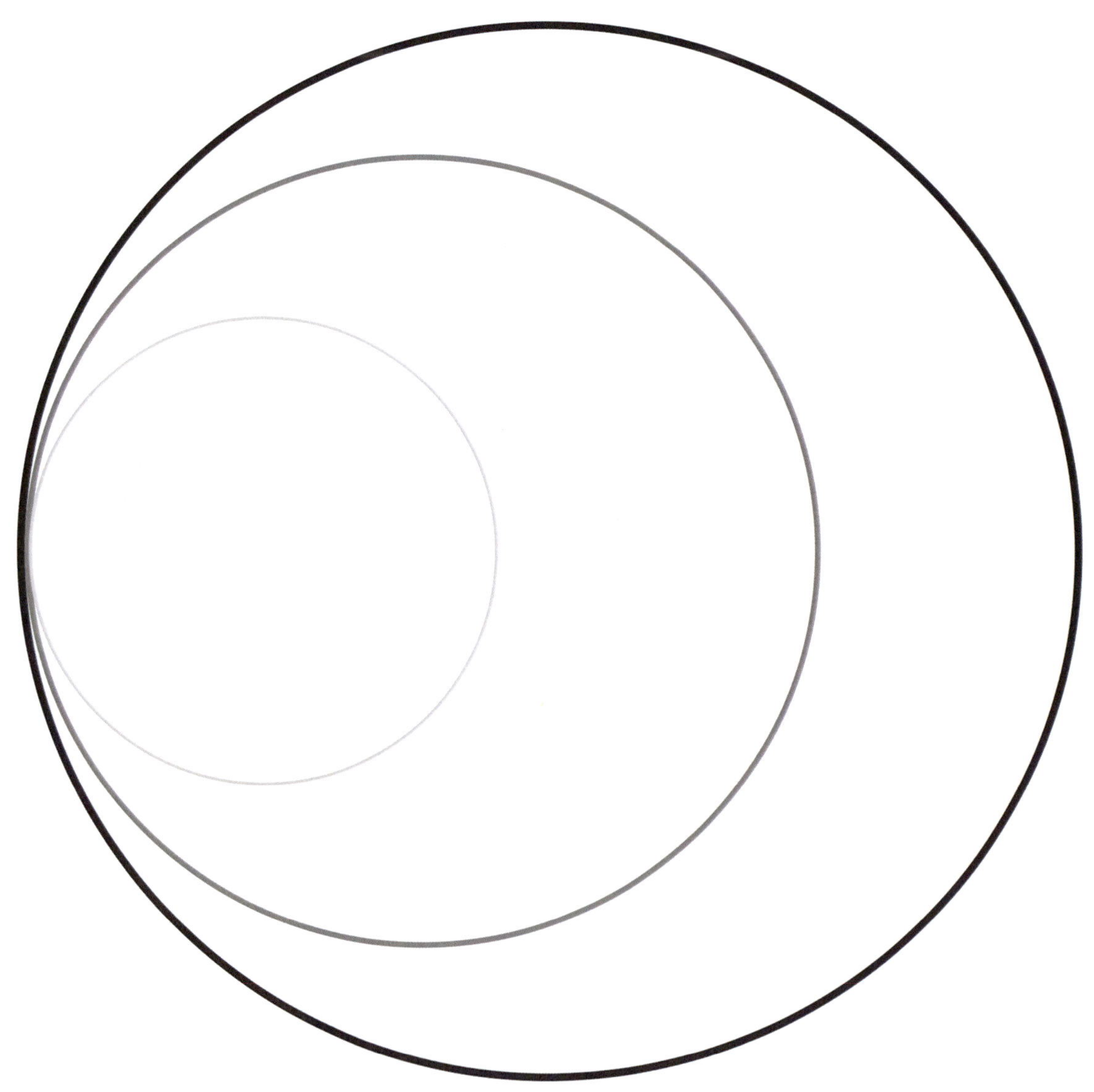

Three Steps of Self Compassion

1. Mindfulness.
2. Common Humanity.
3. Kind Self Talk.

Which of these do you have the most difficulty with?

For most of us, it's talking to ourselves the way we would talk to a friend. Below, write some phrases that you would say to a good friend, a child, or a beloved friend.

Keep these phrases handy to say to yourself during difficult moments.

Kind Self Touch

Try each of the following:

Place a hand on your heart. *Breathe.*

Place a hand on your stomach. *Breathe.*

Place one hand on your heart and one on your stomach. *Breathe.*

Hold your own hand. *Breathe.*

Give yourself a hug. *Breathe.*

Place your hands on your cheeks. *Breathe.*

Return to the touch that felt the most right to you. Repeat the phrases above to yourself.

Your Heart is Invited to Integration:

What would you like to carry forward from this chapter into the days of your life?

Chapter 6: Stuck Between the World You Need to Release and the World You're Afraid to Enter

What is your current version of the Homeless Under a Bridge Game?

What would ACTUALLY have to happen for you to be Homeless Under a Bridge?

What is the cost of NOT taking action?

What do you *need?*

Take a moment to be present to your heart and its wisdom. Let your heart know that you're listening and ask yourself:
"What do I need? What do I truly need?"

This should be a wish for yourself that, if this need is not met on a given day, the day does not feel complete.
This might sound like:

> *May I know that I am loved.*
> *May I rest in my inherent value.*
> *May I be kind to myself.*

Now, close your eyes again and ask your heart a second question:
"What do I need to hear?"

Ask your heart what words it would like to hear if your heart could hear them whispered in your ear every day for the rest of your life.
This might sound like:

> *You're a good person.*
> *You're strong.*
> *You are not alone.*

You can use these phrases as is, or you can turn them into loving kindness phrases:

> *May I know my goodness.*
> *May I feel my strength.*
> *May I see how I am connected with others.*

Find 3-4 phrases that resonate with your heart. Close your eyes and spend a few moments repeating them to yourself, allowing them to settle into your heart. Gently release the phrases, knowing you can return to them at any time.

Noticing the *Breath*

Pause a moment with me.
Scan your physical body. From the very tip top of your head, down through your forehead, the back of your head, your throat and neck, your shoulders and chest, your belly, your upper, mid, and lower back, your hips and thighs, your calves, ankles and feet.

What do you notice? What feels good? What hurts? Where is there pressure? Tightness?

What things are you doing in your life that add to those feelings of tightness and pressure?

Can you breathe even more into the spots that feel tight or sticky?

Can you place a gentle hand on your heart?

What things do you do in your life that help you feel calm, nourished, and connected?

What would your life look like if you did 1% more of those things?

Write about the experience from the previous page & what you've learned.

Your Heart is Invited to Integration:

What would you like to carry forward from
this chapter into the days of your life?

Chapter 7: Spiritual Practices- Prioritizing My Heart and Soul

Your Spiritual Practices

What does your practice of spirituality look like now? How often do you prioritize your heart and soul? What keeps you from doing these more often? What additional spiritual practices would you like to explore? *(Just a reminder that spirituality does not necessarily mean religion!)*

Explore what spiritual practice you'd like to add into your life

Letting Satisfied Be Enough –
The Heart and Soul of an Ordinary Day

How do you know when you're satisfied? What can you do to pause in your day to notice satisfaction, peace, joy, connection?

On the next page, make a collage of photos, quotes, or graphics of things in your day you can pause to notice satisfaction, peace, joy, and connection.

Here is an example

And remember to have fun with it!

Things like my family, sunrises, sunsets, journaling, meditation, eating a good meal, and my pups all foster satisfaction, peace, joy, and connection.

Now its your turn!

Your Heart is Invited to Integration:

What would you like to carry forward from
this chapter into the days of your life?

Chapter 8: Addicted to Action: Spaciousness Rather Than Speed

Comfort Wisdom Layout.

List the things in your life that cause you to numb...

*examples: work stress, relationship stress,
the speed of life with no breaks, boredom...*

Make a representation, with words or pictures, of what you use to numb...

Examples: Food, Exercise, Booze, Sex, Shopping, Doom Scrolling, etc.

Finally, allow yourself ample space to explore your Comfort Wisdom.

Revisit that list of ways that you would like to feel.

What things and activities allow you to experience some of those feelings?
Things like nutritious foods, sleep, movement, music, touch/sex
(the connecting kind), meditation, or yoga.

<u>Create a list of items below</u>

Revisit that list of ways that you would like to feel.

Once you've gotten your representation of the things that bring you true comfort and a sense of spaciousness, take a picture of that list or page in your journal.

Put a copy on your refrigerator or computer, or use it on the backdrop of your phone... any place that can remind you of your comfort wisdom options over numbing.

Any place that can help you connect with your heart with spaciousness over speed.

Your Heart is Invited to Integration:

What would you like to carry forward from
this chapter into the days of your life?

Chapter 9
Integration: Bringing My Head and My Heart into Every Day

*Productive AF -
Put Good Things Into the World
(Head Check)*

♥ What is your version of "easeful creativity"?

♥ How can you bring productive energy into your day without over-functioning and with a sense of ease?

Seasons of Hustle?
(You Better Check Yourself Before You Wreck Yourself!)

How can you plan for your next "season of hustle"?

How can you intentionally create space in your days and in activities
to allow time and space for your heart to breathe?
(As I'm writing this, I'm stepping away for a healthy snack and a little
walk around the cul-de-sac from time to time).

- List out some ideas -

Delighting in Pleasure

What steps can you take to savor pleasure (as well as peace, joy, connection)?

Use the space below to brainstorm steps you can take to savor pleasure

Your Heart is Invited to Integration:

What would you like to carry forward from
this chapter into the days of your life?

Conclusion: Deeper Still

💗 How might you sink into this practice 5% more?

💗 How can you carry your practice forward and go deeper and deeper with each passing moment?

💗 Put a date on your calendar to connect with your heart.

Your Heart is Invited to Integration:

What would you like to carry forward from
this chapter into the days of your life?

A Love Letter to Gen Z

If you're part of Gen Z, how has hustle culture impacted you?

What would you add to a love letter to yourself?

If you're part of a different Generation, what love letter would you write to yourself?

Notes:

Notes:

Gratitudes:

A Deep Thank You to
Lynn McLean
Wendy Jensen
Yiara Blanco
For Your Special Support of this Soul Sabbatical Project

Who and What are You Grateful for?

Join the Soul Sabbatical Community at

www.yolandaharper.com